# THE
# BIG
# FIVE

# THE BIG FIVE

**Shiko Nguru**

Illustrated by
**Michael Machira**

**Collins**

# Contents

# Meet the crew!

**Simba**
Lion – bravery
and leadership

**Elie**
Elephant – smart
and curious

**Rhinoboy**
Rhinocerous – tough
and loyal

**Princess Leopard**
Leopard – athletic
and fierce

**Buff**
Buffalo – no Amazing
Animal Abilities – yet ...

# Nairobi National Park

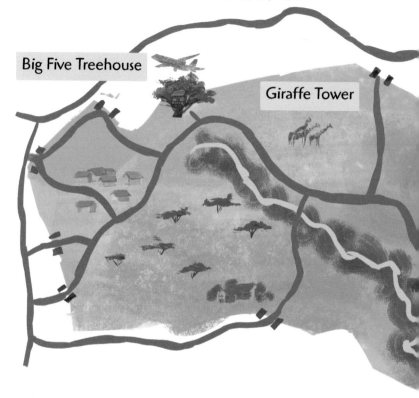

Big Five Treehouse

Giraffe Tower

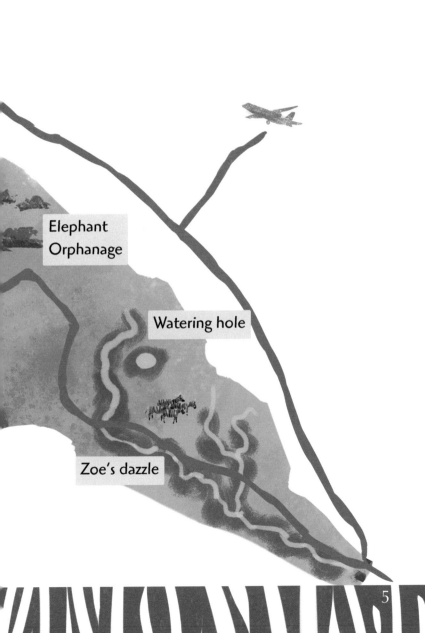

Elephant
Orphanage

Watering hole

Zoe's dazzle

# What are the Big Five?

Africa's "Big Five" is the name given to the five African animals that were once the most difficult and dangerous for a person to hunt. These amazing wild animals still make Africa their home, but these days, visitors photograph them rather than hunt them! They are:

## Lion

Males are larger, but it's the females who often do the hunting.

## Leopard

Leopards tend to live alone and mostly hunt at night.

They are hard to spot because leopards are well-camouflaged!

## Rhinoceros

Rhino's horns are made
of the same material
as our nails!

Their eyesight is poor, so they
rely on their very
strong sense of smell.

## Elephant

Elephants are
the largest land
mammal in
the world!

They can run
quickly, but
can't jump.

## Cape buffalo

Cape buffaloes guard their
homes fiercely.

They're strong swimmers.

# Chapter 1

"Big Five, it's time for treehouse check-in!"
Simba announced. He beamed down at his friends.

Simba always did roll call. He was also the one
who had suggested that they form a junior ranger
team and call themselves the Big Five.

It happened during a school trip to the Nairobi
National Park. The teacher had split the class up
into four groups and asked each group to nominate
a leader.

It was no surprise when the class elected the four
kids who knew the most about Nairobi National Park
as group leaders. All four were children of Kenya
Wildlife Service officers who worked at the park, and
they knew more about its animals than other kids.

After a successful school trip, where nobody
wandered off or got lost, Simba had his great idea.

What if they formed a junior ranger team?

"You mean like a wildlife rescue team?" asked a boy who happened to be eavesdropping on their conversation. He bounced over to where they were standing, his face aglow with excitement.

While Simba was 13-years-old and the other three group leaders were 12, this boy was 11 and a year below them in school. They ran into him often at the park, because he also had a parent who worked there.

Simba considered the boy's suggestion. "I guess we would be like a wildlife rescue team – "

"Then you guys need cool code names!" said the boy.

Simba chuckled. "We could use the names of animals that live here at the park."

Everyone loved the idea.

Simba, the Swahili word for lion, was the perfect name for the eldest member of the team, who they all agreed should be their leader. Just like a lion, Simba was brave and fearless.

The others followed Simba's lead and picked animal names – each with its own strengths. They called these "Triple A's" for Amazing Animal Abilities:

- Simba for lion: bravery and leadership

- Elie for elephant: smart and curious

- Rhinoboy for rhinoceros: tough and loyal

- Princess Leopard: athletic and fierce.

"Hey! These are four of the five animals that make up Africa's famous Big Five!" Simba realised. "The only animal missing is the Buffalo! If only we had a fifth member of the team … then we could call ourselves the Big Five!"

They all turned to the younger boy.

He gulped. "Me? You're asking me to join your wildlife rescue team?"

"Yes!" they chorused.

He looked down. "But … I don't even know what Triple A's a buffalo has – "

"Never mind that," Simba encouraged. "We're happy to have you as part of the team, Buff."

Buff beamed at the sound of his code name. And just like that, the Big Five team was born.

13

Now, six weeks later, they were meeting up for another day of wildlife rescue duties at the park. Starting with team roll call at the treehouse.

"Elie!" Simba called out.

Elie snapped to attention and slapped the elephant badge on her arm. "Present and reporting for duty!"

She made a trumpeting sound as she climbed up to the treehouse.

Simba ticked off her name and let out a loud roar.

Next, he called out the rest of the team codenames: Rhinoboy, Princess Leopard and Buff. They all made different animal sounds – a grunt, a growl and a bellow – before trooping into the treehouse.

Simba marked all members as present and ready for duty.

It was the Big Five's job to patrol the Nairobi National Park and help protect its wildlife.

"What are our duties for today?" Rhinoboy asked, rubbing his hands together. He knew that there was no shortage of jobs to be done.

Simba flipped over a page on his clipboard. "We have a few baby animals to check up on. Let's see."

Princess Leopard jerked her head, nearly losing her headpiece. This colourful, beaded ornament was often worn by royalty in the past, and was the reason why everyone called her Princess. She wore the traditional crown, a gift from her grandmother, proudly every single day.

"Oh, I know!" Princess Leopard exclaimed. "A giraffe gave birth to a calf last night! My mum told me about it on the way in."

Princess Leopard's mum was a vet at the park.

"Yup!" Simba confirmed. "The newest member of the Giraffe Tower was born late last night, and we need to check it's OK."

"Giraffe Tower?" asked Buff. "What's that?"

Rhinoboy grinned. "It's another name for a herd of giraffes. Isn't that cool? Whoever came up with that must have been thinking about how tall they are!"

17

"Probably," smiled Simba. "Then we need to visit the Elephant Orphanage, before we check on the zebra herd. We need to make sure the zebra foals are ready for their migration."

"That's right!" said Rhinoboy. "Now it's the rainy season, it's time for them to migrate to the plains!"

Buff scrunched his nose. "Why do some animals do that?"

"Because the bushes grow big in the rainy season, meaning predators can easily hunt down the zebra. So the zebra travel to the wide, open plains where it's safer."

Rhinoboy jumped up. "What are we waiting for? Let's get to it!"

With hands on their badges and chins held high,
the team recited their motto:

Animals deserve our respect,

so we explore, discover and protect!

# Chapter 2

"All set?" Kip asked, glancing behind to make sure all five junior rangers were safely inside the safari car.

Nairobi National Park was home to a large wildlife population and with many wild animals roaming about, one of the park's most important rules was to stay inside the safari vehicles at all times.

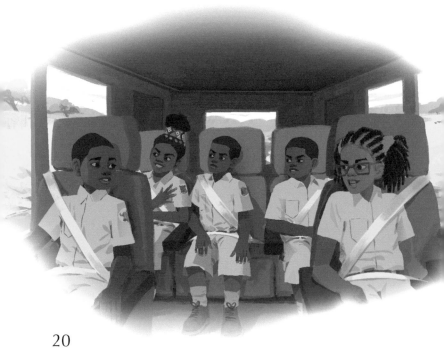

"Here we go!" Kip, one of the park rangers, boomed as he started the car. They were headed towards the first stop on their tour: the Giraffe Tower.

"Look!" Princess Leopard exclaimed, pointing at the water hole. "I see the giraffes … and … the calf!"

Kip brought the safari car as close to the tower as he could, without startling the animals.

"That's a newborn giraffe? She's huge!" Buff marvelled.

"Newborn giraffes are around 1.8 metres tall and weigh over 50 kilograms!" exclaimed Kip.

Buff shook his head in amazement. "I can't believe she was born yesterday and she's running around already!"

"Yup, she looks healthy and strong," Simba agreed as he ticked off the first item on their duty chart.

"Here's a fun fact!" Rhinoboy chirped. "Giraffe mums give birth standing up! That means their calves drop almost two metres to the ground when they're born! The fall shocks them into action, so they're up and running in no time!"

Princess Leopard grabbed a camera from the safari car. "I'll take some photos – my mum's going to want to know how the calf is doing!"

After Princess Leopard snapped as many photos of the speedy giraffe as she could, they waved goodbye to the Giraffe Tower and continued to their next stop – the Elephant Orphanage.

The Big Five arrived just in time. The elephant calves they'd come to see were about to leave! They rushed out of the safari car and began taking turns feeding them from two large milk bottles.

"Where are these calves going?" Buff wondered.

"It's time for Naliana and Savarra to go and live with other elephants in the wild," Simba answered.

The elephant keeper taking care of the two calves flashed a proud smile. "Yup! Remember how small and scared they were when they joined us at the orphanage three years ago? Now look at them – playful and confident, ready to take on the world!"

"Naliana and Savarra were rescued as newborns, after their mums were killed by poachers who wanted their tusks," Elie explained to Buff.

Rhinoboy sighed. "It's sad that so many elephants end up orphaned because of poachers."

The keeper agreed. "That's why the work all of us do here at the park is so important. Taking care of elephants that can't take care of themselves is good, and creating safe, natural habitats for them so they can live happily in the wild, is even better."

Elie turned to Buff. "This park is too small, so the calves are being transferred to a larger wildlife reserve where they can live safely with other elephants."

Simba checked off the second item on their to-do list as Naliani and Savarra walked into the large transport vehicle.

"Happy release day!" The Big Five shouted and waved as the truck exited the orphanage gates.

Princess Leopard clapped excitedly. "Time to go see if Zelda, Zain and Zoe are ready for the migration!"

Besides spotty leopards, striped zebras were Princess Leo's favourite animals.

"I see the dazzle!" Princess Leopard shouted.

"Dazzle?" Buff asked.

"A dazzle of zebras is –" Rhinoboy began.

"Let me guess," Buff interrupted, half smiling. "A dazzle is a cool word to use instead of 'herd' for a group of zebras?"

The others laughed as they bobbed their heads.

The safari car pulled up close enough for them to have a better look at the zebras. Then, through their binoculars, they carefully searched for the foals.

"I see Zain!" Elie exclaimed. "And over there, look, it's Zelda!"

Buff shook his head. "They all look the same to me. How can you tell who's who?!"

"Every zebra has a unique stripe pattern. Just like human fingerprints, no two zebras are the same," Princess Leopard answered.

Rhinoboy pointed a finger into the air. "Another fun fact about zebras is that only their fur is striped. Underneath, their skin is plain black, and they look like horses. Also, just so you know, their fur is black with white stripes, not the other way around."

Buff's eyebrows shot up. He had always thought that zebras were white with black stripes!

"Um, guys?" Simba interrupted. "I can't see Zoe anywhere."

Kip moved in closer so they could check every stripe, but Zoe was nowhere to be found. Kip wore a grim look on his face. "Nope. She's not here."

"Where could she be?" Princess Leopard panicked.

Simba's face clouded with concern. "I don't know, but we have to find her, because if Zoe doesn't get back to the herd before sundown, they'll migrate without her."

Buff gulped. "What … what happens if she gets left behind?"

"Zoe's only seven months old," Elie answered gravely. "Alone in the park, without the rest of the dazzle to look after her, she'll be easy prey for predators like lions and cheetahs."

"We can't let that happen!" Princess Leopard cried.

"We won't," Simba reassured her. "Big Five, we have a mission. Our mission is to find Zoe and bring her back to the herd. Before it's too late!"

# Chapter 3

Back at the treehouse, Simba pulled out a map of the Nairobi National Park. "The park has electric fences on the north, east and west sides. The south is left open so that the animals can migrate back and forth when they need to."

Rhinoboy gnawed on a fingertip. His eyes were narrowed in thought. "We don't have time to search the whole park ... we need to stick to areas where Zoe is most likely to go."

"What about here?" Princess Leopard asked, pointing to a cluster of trees on the map.

Elie shook her head. "No, that area's too wooded. Plain zebras like Zoe stick to the wide, open plains so they can keep an eye out for predators."

"OK, so we look for Zoe in places that don't have a lot of trees," Princess Leopard said. "That still leaves a lot of ground to cover before sundown."

"I think this map can help us narrow it down," said Simba. "Look." He crossed out all the forests on the map. He then drew three large circles covering areas with no trees. "She could be in any of these circled areas."

Buff pointed at one of the circles. "Why does it say 'Poacher Watch Area' on that side of the map?"

"It means there have been incidents of poaching reported in that area," Princess Leopard said worriedly. "The park rangers keep a special look out for poachers there, to make sure the animals are safe. But the rangers can't be there the whole time! If Zoe is there, she could be hunted for her beautiful coat, or even her meat. Some people believe that zebra meat is special and can cure diseases."

Elie shook her head again. "I don't think Zoe could have travelled that far. Plus, she would have had to go through these wooded patches to get there. She's more likely to be in one of these other two circles." She pointed at the two large, open areas without many trees.

Simba crossed out one of the circles on the map. "Right. That still leaves us with two large areas to search," he said determinedly. "We need to narrow it down to one."

The Big Five chewed nervously on their packed lunches as they thought about this. With only one car and not nearly enough time, they had to decide where to search, quickly.

Maybe we're thinking about it the wrong way," Rhinoboy suggested. "Instead of asking where Zoe would go, we should be asking *why* she would go there in the first place."

"Good question!" Princess Leopard chirped, snapping her fingers. "Why would Zoe leave the herd?"

"It's especially weird because zebras are social animals," Elie said. "They like to live together in small family groups."

"So ... why would Zoe run away from her dazzle, her family?" Simba puzzled.

"Could a predator have scared her off?" Buff asked.

"Not likely – " Rhinoboy replied, tilting his head. "Foals, especially those as young as Zoe, are protected by the whole herd. The other zebras wouldn't let a predator get close enough to her to scare her away."

"What about food? Could she have wandered off looking for something to eat?" Simba wondered out loud once again.

"No … Zoe is still really young. She would go to her mum for milk if she was hungry," Elie reasoned.

"Well, something made her run away!" said Princess Leopard.

"What if – " Buff started to ask in a small voice. "What if she was scared … you know, of the migration?"

A few seconds passed as they considered Buff's suggestion.

Elie spoke first. "The wildebeest, gazelles and a few zebras have started to migrate already. Zoe could have figured out what was happening."

Princess Leopard's eyes widened. "And this is her first migration ... she might have been afraid of leaving the only home she's ever known!"

"That's why she ran away! So she wouldn't have to leave home!" Simba added. "Good thinking, Buff!"

Buff couldn't help but smile as the others nodded their approval.

"If Zoe left the dazzle because she was afraid of leaving the park … leaving her home … where would she go?" Rhinoboy asked.

Buff smiled shyly. "When I'm going to a new place that seems scary, I like to hold onto something that reminds me of home. It's why I carried my blankie to school with me on the first day of school."

"Zoe might have gone somewhere that felt like home to her," Princess Leopard offered.

Rhinoboy blew a raspberry in frustration. "Zebras roam around all the time, so Zoe's home could be anywhere in the park!"

Elie jumped up. "But Zoe's only seven months old! She hasn't had time to explore the whole park yet. Just like Buff's blankie reminded him of home, she would most likely go somewhere she spent time as a newborn. Somewhere she knows."

Simba jabbed his finger at one of the two circles left on the map. "Like here! The area where she was born!"

Princess Leopard pumped her fists into the air, then yanked Buff up onto his feet and proudly announced: "Great job, Buff!"

"Come on, everyone!" Rhinoboy yelled, already scrambling down the steps of the treehouse. "Let's go and find Zoe the runaway zebra!"

# Chapter 4

Kip drove through the park and parked the safari car in the centre of a wide grassy area.

"Here we are!" announced Kip. "Zoe's mum gave birth to her in this part of the park seven months ago."

The Big Five searched the area with their binoculars, looking for signs of Zoe.

"Look over there!" Elie suddenly shouted. "It's an animal highway!"

The others followed her pointed finger to a well-worn path that wound through the tall grass. It looked like a dirt hiking trail only much more narrow and harder to see unless you knew what you were looking for.

It was no wonder that Elie was the first to see the highway, as her Triple A was to be smart and curious. That meant she was great at spotting and sniffing out clues.

"An animal highway is a natural path made by wild animals as they move from one part of the park to another," Simba said to Buff. "There's a good chance Zoe is travelling along this trail."

The safari car crawled forward slowly, alongside the trail. "Do you guys smell that?" Elie asked, looking around.

Princess Leopard wrinkled her nose. "It smells like scat – animal droppings."

"Right there!" Rhinoboy exclaimed. "I see the scat!"

Elie clapped her hands excitedly. "Perfect!"

Buff used two fingers to pinch his nostrils shut. "What's so great about finding stinky animal poo?" he asked in a nasally voice.

"Scat can tell us a lot about the animal that left it," Kip explained as the car stopped in front of a pile of animal droppings.

"Zoe's scat should be made up of round, medium-sized, black droppings," Rhinoboy said.

Princess Leopard sighed. "These droppings are smaller than they should be. And instead of being round, these are a funny shape, and they look like have a dent on one side. I don't think this is zebra scat."

Just then, they heard the sound of rustling and heavy breathing coming from a nearby bush. It sounded like an animal was in distress.

Kip pulled forward so they could investigate. "Oh no!" Princess Leopard cried. "That giraffe's got its neck tangled up in a rubbish bag!"

The giraffe was bent over and thrashing around, trying to break free, but the more it struggled, the more tangled it became.

47

"That must have been giraffe scat back there. The dent in giraffe droppings comes from landing on the ground from so high up," Kip explained. "And it looks like the same giraffe got trapped while trying to feed from this bush."

Kip pulled a penknife from his pocket. "I've had to do this before. Litter left by humans is becoming a big problem for wildlife at the park. You guys stay here. I'll be right back."

Slowly, Kip eased out of the car and inched toward the giraffe. It was against park rules to approach animals, but exceptions were made when the animals were in danger. To be safe, Rhinoboy stepped out of the car too and stood guard, looking around protectively in case of any predators. His Triple A was that he was tough and loyal. That made him a great guard and protector – just like a rhinoceros.

While Kip sliced through the rubbish bag, Simba ran over and helped to ease its neck free of the tangled plastic. He looked confident as he tugged gently at its neck, reminding them all that, just like a lion, his Triple A was bravery and leadership. In no time, the giraffe was free. It immediately took off running back down the trail.

Simba was on his way back to the vehicle when he noticed something on the ground. "Guys, I see hoof tracks! And they're going the other way … away from the bush!"

"What do they look like?" Elie called out.

"They're an oval shape with what looks like a triangle cut out of the bottom," Simba replied.

"Those come from animals with single-toed hooves, like horses and zebras!" Princess Leopard shrieked.

"There are no horses at the park so those must be zebra prints," Rhinoboy added, walking over to Simba. "And they look small, so this must have come from a foal!"

"Where does the trail lead?" Buff asked eagerly.

"Animal highways usually lead to sources of food or water," Simba replied, as he and Rhinoboy climbed back into the safari car.

After a short drive following the tracks, Kip stopped. "We have a problem, kids. This animal highway ends here. And so do the hoof prints."

"That's probably because there are multiple food and water sources from here on out," Elie said sadly. "Zoe could have gone in any direction."

"Then how will we know where to go?" Buff asked.

"I think I have an idea," Princess Leopard said. "Could you bring the car up against that tree?"

When Kip stopped the car underneath a large acacia tree, Princess Leopard quickly reached up, grabbed hold of a thick branch and hoisted herself up.

She was an excellent gymnast, and her Triple A was to be athletic and fierce. That meant she could scale trees in seconds, just like a leopard.

Princess Leopard looked across the horizon, scanning back and forth with her binoculars a few times, then gasped. "I think I see something!"

# Chapter 5

"There she is!" Princess Leopard yelled. "There's Zoe!"

Princess Leo quickly climbed down and jumped back into the safari car, guiding Kip towards an area filled with tall grass. Sure enough, right there, standing stock still in the middle of it, was Zoe the zebra.

"We found her!" Buff said a little too loudly.

"Shhhhh!" Simba hushed. "She's sleeping and we don't want to scare her off."

Buff squeezed his eyebrows together. "How can she be asleep? She's standing up!"

"Yup, zebras sleep while standing. It keeps them semi-alert so they can escape from predators if they need to," Elie answered.

Kip turned off the engine a safe distance away as the Big Five watched Zoe through their binoculars. She was very, very still.

"This is perfect," Simba whispered. "Because she's so still, it'll be much easier to tranquillise her."

The car's two-way radio crackled to life as Kip spoke into it. "Requesting assistance for animal transport," he said.

He then pulled out a toolbox from underneath his seat and popped it open to reveal a dart gun. "I'm going to tranquillise Zoe now so that she's ready for pick up when the transport team arrives," he informed the team.

The Big Five watched as Kip crept forward and crouched behind a large rock. While Zoe was still standing statue-still, he positioned the dart gun, aiming directly for her shoulder blade, and applied the tranquilliser to her shoulder. They watched as the tranquilliser hit her skin, making Zoe flinch before slumping into a seated position.

"Is she OK?" Buff asked worriedly after a few minutes had gone by.

Simba nodded. "Tranquillisers are used to calm animals for transport … and look, here comes her ride." A pick-up truck with two rangers slowed down as it drove past their safari car.

"Hi Mum!" Buff called out.

"Hi Dad!" Rhinoboy added.

The adults waved, hopping out of the truck. "Good job tracking Zoe, Big Five!" they said, smiling proudly at them.

They pulled up next to Zoe, then Buff's mum grabbed a thick sheet of plastic from the bed of the truck, while Rhinoboy's dad approached Zoe with a large piece of cloth. He carefully used it to cover Zoe's eyes.

"Blindfolds stop animals from getting scared while humans are handling them," Simba murmured before Buff could ask.

Zoe was relaxed and calm as the two rangers eased her onto the plastic sheet that was laid out on the grass. Her breathing was slow and even, almost as if she was still sleeping.

When the rangers took out their phones and started to take photos of Zoe, Buff threw up his hands impatiently. "Mum!" he blustered. "There's no time for photos! If we don't hurry up, Zoe's going to miss the migration!"

Rhinoboy's dad chuckled. "We're not taking pictures for fun, we're taking them so we can keep track of Zoe. The photos will make sure every ranger in Kenya knows what Zoe looks like, so we'll all be able to recognise her, whether she's here at the park or over at the plains."

"Tracking animals is an important part of wildlife conservation because it keeps us informed of their movements and behaviours. The more we know about animals, the better equipped we are to protect them," Buff's mum explained.

The Big Five nudged each other and slapped their arm badges. "Animals deserve our respect, so we explore, discover and protect!"

Both the rangers laughed. "That's right!" Rhinoboy's dad chimed. "And to protect zebras like Zoe, we track each one by using their unique stripes like barcodes. We're taking photos of Zoe's stripes, or her 'barcode', so we can log her into our database."

Simba's face lit up. "Your animal tracking machine is like a supermarket barcode scanner, only yours scans the stripes on zebras!" he exclaimed.

61

"Exactly!" said Buff's mum. "Anyone in the park can use their phone to scan Zoe and find out all they need to know about her."

"That's so cool!" Buff marvelled, beaming.

When they were finished taking photos, they lifted the sheet and put Zoe in the back of their truck. "All done, Zoe ... logged and loaded!" Rhinoboy's dad concluded.

"Are zebras the only animals you photograph for the database?" Elie asked.

"Right now, yes," Rhinoboy's dad answered. "But we're looking at rolling out the same technology for other animals with one-of-a-kind patterns, like giraffes … and leopards too."

"Super cool!" Princess Leopard cheered.

The safari car started off after the slow-moving pick-up truck.

Buff relaxed back into his seat. "Whew! We found Zoe in time. Our mission is complete!"

"Not yet," Simba said. "We have to see it through to the very end. That means getting Zoe back to her dazzle in time for the migration."

The sky was turning orange with sunset as they moved along the bumpy road in the direction of the zebra dazzle.

"Can't they drive any faster?" Princess Leopard whined.

"They can't risk injuring Zoe," Rhinoboy replied. Though he was biting his nails and sneaking worried glances at his watch too.

"What if … What if we're too late? What if Zoe's dazzle has already gone? What if she's missed the migration?" Buff quivered.

The rest of the Big Five dropped their eyes, too afraid to answer.

# Chapter 6

The safari car followed the pick-up truck all the way back to the spot where the Big Five last saw Zoe's dazzle, but the zebras were nowhere to be found.

"We're too late," Buff moaned.

"Not so fast, I have an idea!" Elie piped up. "Let's check by the water hole!"

Simba snapped his fingers. "Great idea! They need to refuel before they start their journey."

Rhinoboy nodded his head. "So ... the zebras went to the water hole to have a good, long drink for the last time and maybe eat some nutrient-rich grass before the migration?"

"Like a pitstop for snacks before a road trip!" Buff added.

Kip started the engine back up. "Yup. And it's an idea worth checking out." He immediately radioed for the pick-up truck to follow them in the direction of the nearest watering hole.

As it often turned out, Elie was right. Around the water hole was the dazzling sight of zebras drinking their fill of cool, fresh water. It was Zoe's dazzle!

"We did it!" Princess Leopard cheered, giving the others high fives. "We got Zoe back to her family in time for the migration!"

Simba smiled proudly. "Job well done, Big Five."

They looked on as the two rangers lifted Zoe out of the pick-up, lowered her onto the grass and removed her blindfold. The tranquilliser had clearly worn off because Zoe was up in a flash and galloping in the direction of the zebras

"How will she find her mum?" Buff asked, as Zoe weaved her way through dozens of zebras.

"From when they're newborns, zebras learn to identify their mums by their stripes, their smell and even the sounds they make," Simba explained.

Rhinoboy pointed. "Yes, it's called imprinting, and look, Zoe's found her!"

The Big Five beamed as they watched. Zoe neighed excitedly as she nuzzled up to a larger zebra.

Then, as if they had only been waiting for Zoe to arrive, the zebras began to move. It was slow at first, but soon grew into a steady run in the direction of the plains. The migration was underway.

"Will Zoe be OK?" Buff worried.

Princess Leopard patted his back. "Migrations can be dangerous, but zebras have things that help keep them safe … like their stripes which camouflage them in the tall grass."

"They can also give a mean kick and bite when they have to," Rhinoboy added.

"Or snort to warn each other when danger is near," Simba finished off.

"Sounds like Zoe has some handy Triple A's that'll keep her safe," said Buff.

A huge cloud of dust was left billowing behind the zebras as they stampeded across the grassland.

"I'm going to miss them," Buff sighed, as they started the drive back to the treehouse.

"Don't worry, they'll be back next season," Elie said, trying to cheer him up.

"But what if they get lost on the way back to the park?" Buff asked.

Rhinoboy shook his head. "They won't. Migrating animals just seem to know where to go!"

"Yup, you don't need to worry, Buff. Because zebras always find their way back to our park," Princess Leopard confirmed.

"Big Five, it's time for treehouse check-out!" Simba announced. He held out his clipboard and prepared to call out from their duty chart.

"Welfare check on newborn giraffe?"

Princess Leopard perked up. "Check! Giraffe calf was confirmed to be healthy and standing tall."

"More like running around like a crazy chicken," Buff giggled.

Simba laughed too as he moved onto the next item on the chart.

"Elephant calf release day?"

"Check!" Rhinoboy shouted. "Naliani and Savarra have been released from the orphanage and are on their way to live with other elephants in the wild."

"Can you imagine leaving school at only three years old?" Princess Leopard mused.

The others shook their heads, trying to imagine moving out of home while still a toddler.

"And last but certainly not least," Simba continued, "finding Zoe the runaway Zebra!"

Elie pumped both fists in the air. "Check! We found Zoe and safely brought her back to the dazzle in time for the migration."

"We also freed that giraffe caught in the rubbish bag," Buff reminded them.

Simba scribbled with his pencil. "That's right! Bonus duty: Giraffe rescue," he said before checking it off too.

He unclipped the duty chart and presented it to Buff. "It was you who gave us the first clue to accomplishing our mission of finding Zoe. You're quick on your feet, just like a real-life buffalo. That's your Triple A, Buff! So you should do the honours and pin this up."

Buff could barely contain his pride. He had a Triple A just like the others! His smile stretched from ear to ear as he pinned the day's completed duty chart next to the other sheets of paper on the Big Five victory wall. Being a junior ranger was the best thing in the world!

This time, it was him who slapped his buffalo animal badge first. The others shot up to stand beside him, and with the proud satisfaction of a successful day swelling their chests, they shouted out the Big Five motto together:

Animals deserve our respect,
so we explore, discover and protect!

# The Great Migration in Africa

A migration is when animals travel from one area to another.

The wildebeest migration is so large it can be seen from space!

# Animal groups

Do you know the names for groups of these animals? They may not be what you think!

| individual | group |
|---|---|
| lion | pride |
| hyena | cackle |
| rhinoceros | crash |

| individual | group |
|---|---|
| zebra | dazzle |
| giraffe | tower |
| elephant | memory |
| buffalo | herd |

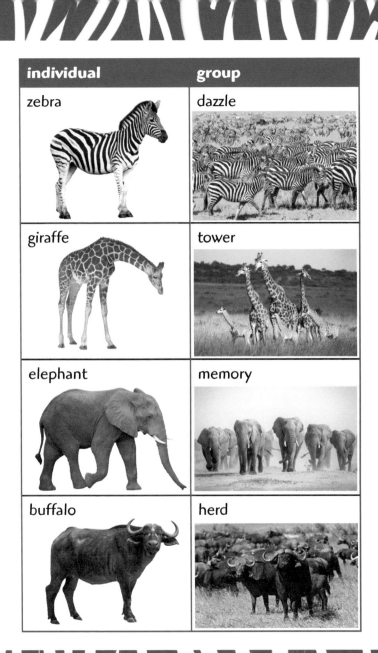

# Safari rules

If you're going on safari, it's really important that you keep the following rules in mind:

**1** Do not try to feed the animals, they're wild creatures!

**2** Stay in the car at all times. Remember, this isn't a zoo!

**3** Animals can get scared very easily, so keep your voice down and try to make as little noise as possible.

**4** Don't litter, it's important to keep the environment in the same way you found it!

**5** Finally, always listen to the guide, they're the experts.

# Learn some Swahili!

Simba

Lion

Jambo

Hello

Chui

Leopard

Safari

Safari

Kifaru

Rhinoceros

Tembo

Elephant

# About the author

**How did you get into writing?**
I was looking for a way to teach my daughter about east Africa in a way that was fun and exciting. Since I couldn't find any books that told stories about our nature, wildlife and history in a way that she could enjoy, I decided to write some myself!

**Shiko Nguru**

**What do you hope readers will get out of the book?**
I hope that readers will enjoy learning about the beauty of the wild and how important it is to protect and preserve it.

**Is there anything in this book that relates to your own experiences?**
When I was around 8 years old, I wanted to be a wildlife ranger!

**What is it like for you to write?**
Writing is hard work because it takes a lot of perseverance to keep going long enough to get an idea out of your head and onto the page. That being said, I love the process of coming up with characters and plotlines, and then weaving them together to create stories that others can enjoy.

**What is a book you remember loving reading when you were young?**

*The Famous Five* books by Enid Blyton (I think I read all of them!)

**Why did you want to write this book?**

I think sometimes we forget how beautiful our planet is and how precious our wild animals are. My hope is that this book serves as a little reminder!

**Have you seen any of the Big Five animals in real life?**

Yes – all of them! Growing up in Kenya, we went for school trips to the national park almost every year in primary school.

**If you were one of the Big Five team, what would your animal name and Triple A be?**

Lioness! Triple A: protective and hardworking.

**Do you have any advice for children who want to help look after wildlife?**

Yes! Explore – take every opportunity to visit wild animals in their natural environments, Discover – learn as much about wildlife and matters affecting them as you can, and then Protect – look for ways you can help make our planet safer and healthier for wild animals.

# About the illustrator

**What made you want to be an illustrator?**

I have always enjoyed drawing
because it is a way to experience and
then express the imaginary world.
I discovered that I enjoy the process
of drawing and telling stories
through illustration.

**How did you get
into illustration?**

I got into illustration by following

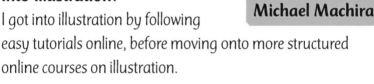

Michael Machira

easy tutorials online, before moving onto more structured
online courses on illustration.

**What did you like best about illustrating this book?**

There are many highlights to illustrating this book.
What I liked the most was drawing the characters and,
through them, experiencing their adventure.

**What was the most difficult thing about illustrating
this book?**

The most difficult thing about illustrating this book was
trying to capture the image in my mind through drawings
while still fulfilling the objective of the illustration.

**Is there anything in this book that relates to your own experiences?**

When I was young, our primary school took us on a trip to various places – among them the Nairobi National Park. This book reminds me of the magical feeling of being introduced to different animals, their characteristics, and behaviours.

**How do you bring a character to life in an illustration?**

I bring a character to life in an illustration by reading as much as I can find on the character, and then researching information that may reveal more about the character. Finally, I sit back and imagine the character's habits and life before making sketches. With this background work done, it becomes easier to figure out how a character would express themselves in different situations.

**Which character or scene did you most like illustrating?**

The scene I most liked illustrating is where Princess Leopard is looking out into the horizon through the binoculars while atop a tree.

**What's your favourite animal to draw?**

A zebra.

# Book chat

Which character did you like best, and why?

Did your mood change while you were reading the book? If so, how?

If you could change one thing about this book, what would it be?

If you had to give the book a new title, what would you choose?

Which part of the book did you like best, and why?

Is there an animal in particular you'd like to see if you went on a safari?

Which scene stands out most for you? Why?

What animal would you choose as your ranger name and what is your Triple A?

**Book challenge:**
Think of some ways you could help protect the wildlife around you!

**Collins**
**BIG CAT**

Published by Collins
An imprint of HarperCollins*Publishers*

The News Building
1 London Bridge Street
London SE1 9GF
UK

Macken House
39/40 Mayor Street Upper
Dublin 1
D01 C9W8
Ireland

10 9 8 7 6 5 4 3

ISBN 978-0-00-862486-6

British Library Cataloguing-in-Publication
Data
A catalogue record for this publication is
available from the British Library.

Download the teaching notes and
word cards to accompany this book at:
http://littlewandle.org.uk/signupfluency/

**Get the latest Collins Big Cat news at**
collins.co.uk/collinsbigcat

Author: Shiko Nguru
Illustrator: Michael Machira (Shannon Associates)
Publisher: Lizzie Catford
Product manager: Caroline Green
Series editor: Charlotte Raby
Commissioning editor and
    content editor: Daniela Mora Chavarría
Development editor: Catherine Baker
Project manager: Emily Hooton
Copyeditor: Catherine Dakin
Proofreader: Gaynor Spry
Cover designer: Sarah Finan
Typesetter: 2Hoots Publishing Services Ltd
Production controller: Katharine Willard

Collins would like to thank the teachers and children at the
following schools who took part in the trialling of Big Cat
for Little Wandle Fluency: Burley And Woodhead Church of
England Primary School; Chesterton Primary School; Lady
Margaret Primary School; Little Sutton Primary School;
Parsloes Primary School.

Printed and bound in the UK

**MIX**
Paper | Supporting
responsible forestry
**FSC**
www.fsc.org   **FSC™ C007454**

This book is produced from independently
certified FSC™ paper to ensure
responsible forest management.

For more information visit:
www.harpercollins.co.uk/green

Acknowledgements
The publishers gratefully acknowledge the permission granted
to reproduce the copyright material in this book. Every effort
has been made to trace copyright holders and to obtain their
permission for the use of copyright material. The publishers
will gladly receive any information enabling them to rectify
any error or omission at the first opportunity.

p6 Eric Isselee/Shutterstock, p7t Philippe Clement/
Shutterstock, p7c Four Oaks/Shutterstock, p7b GoodFocused/
Shutterstock, p78 Mcknub/Shutterstock, p79 Gudkov Andrey/
Shutterstock, p80tl Eric Isselee/Shutterstock, p80tr AfriPics.
com/Alamy, p80cl Krakenimages.com/Shutterstock, p80cr
Abdelrahman Hassanein/Shutterstock, p80bl Steve Collender/
Shutterstock, p80br Martin Harvey/Alamy, p81tl Jan Martin
Will/Shutterstock, p81tr GranTotufo/Shutterstock, p81tcl Eric
Isselee/Shutterstock, p81tcr Craig Fraser/Shutterstock, p81bcl
gualtiero boffi/Shutterstock, p81bcr Stu Porter/Shutterstock,
p81bl Benny Marty/Shutterstock, p81br kyslynskahal/
Shutterstock, p82t Eric Isselee/Shutterstock, p82b Pedro Helder
Pinheiro/Shutterstock, p83 Yaroslav Astakhov/Shutterstock,
p84 Eric Isselee/Shutterstock, p85t Philippe Clement/
Shutterstock, p85b Four Oaks/Shutterstock.